VOCAL SOLO

SOLOS FROM MUSICALS FOR KIDS

COMPILED BY LOUISE LERCH

To access companion recorded performances and accompaniments online, visit:
www.halleonard.com/mylibrary

8507-1356-9326-8186

ISBN 978-0-7935-8227-3

HAL•LEONARD®
CORPORATION
7777 W. BLUEMOUND RD. P.O. BOX 13819 MILWAUKEE, WI 53213

Visit Hal Leonard Online at
www.halleonard.com

SOLOS FROM MUSICALS FOR KIDS

CONTENTS

Children Singers, prepared by Louise Lerch:
[1] Amanda Addison, age 11
[2] Katharine Chambers, age 12
[3] Katie Chu, age 9
[4] Amber Edmunds, age 11
[5] Joe Westergard, age 11

Pianist on Recordings: Louise Lerch

The price of this publication includes access to companion recorded performances and accompaniments online, for download or streaming, using the unique code printed on the title page.
Visit **www.halleonard.com/mylibrary** and enter the access code.

THE BARE NECESSITIES
from Walt Disney's THE JUNGLE BOOK

Words and Music by
TERRY GILKYSON

BEAUTY AND THE BEAST
from Walt Disney's BEAUTY AND THE BEAST

Lyrics by HOWARD ASHMAN
Music by ALAN MENKEN

Lyrically

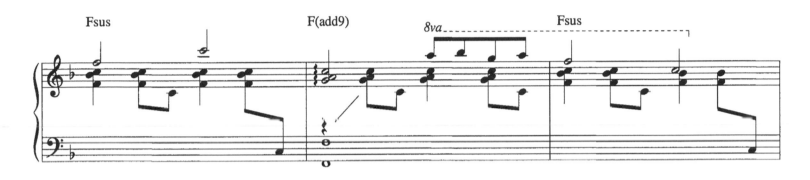

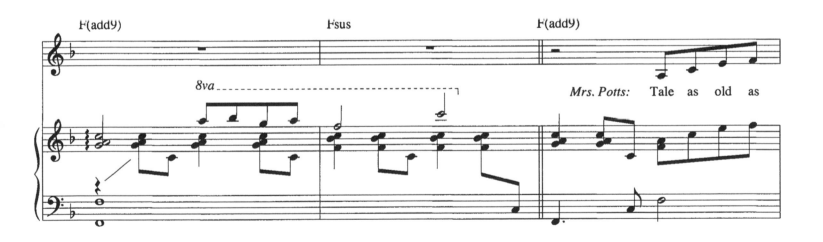

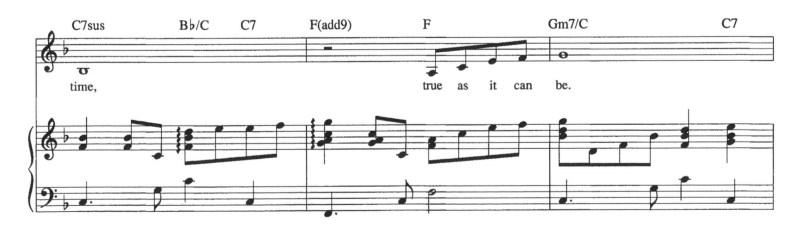

BE KIND TO YOUR PARENTS

from FANNY

Words and Music by
HAROLD ROME

BORN TO ENTERTAIN
from RUTHLESS

Lyrics by JOEL PALEY
Music by MARVIN LAIRD

Some girls like __ to cook and sew; __ When I cook it's in a show. __ I was born to en- ter- tain. __

spoken to audience: "How ya doin'?" Some girls pre- fer to

*Pocatello (pronounced Pocatella) is a town in Idaho.

COUNT YOUR BLESSINGS INSTEAD OF SHEEP

from the Motion Picture Irving Berlin's WHITE CHRISTMAS

Words and Music by
IRVING BERLIN

GARY, INDIANA

from Meredith Willson's THE MUSIC MAN

By MEREDITH WILLSON

I WHISTLE A HAPPY TUNE

from THE KING AND I

Lyrics by OSCAR HAMMERSTEIN II
Music by RICHARD RODGERS

Moderately

mf

p

Bb

Bb9

When - ev - er I feel a - fraid I

Eb

F7

hold my head e - rect And whis - tle a hap - py

F7#5 **Bb**

F7

tune, so no one will sus - pect I'm a -

PART OF YOUR WORLD
from Walt Disney's THE LITTLE MERMAID

Lyrics by HOWARD ASHMAN
Music by ALAN MENKEN

Moderately bright

Look at this stuff. __ Is - n't it neat? __

Would-n't you think __ my col - lec-tion's com-plete? Would-n't you think __ I'm the girl, __

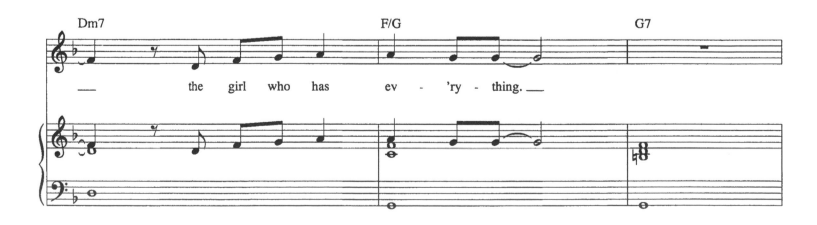

__ the girl who has ev - 'ry - thing. __

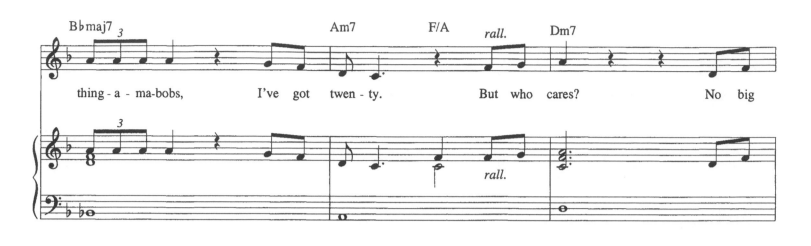

thing-a-ma-bobs, I've got twen-ty. But who cares? No big

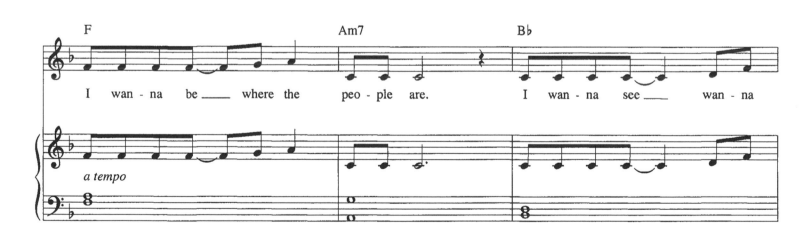

deal. I want more.

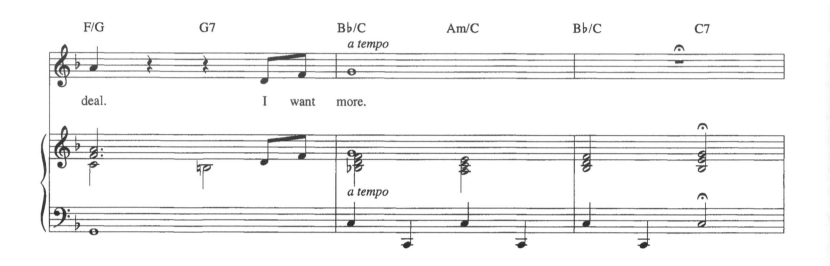

I wan-na be ___ where the peo-ple are. I wan-na see ___ wan-na

see 'em danc-in', walk-in' a-round ___ on those, what-d-ya call ___ 'em, oh

out of the sea.

Wish I could

be

part of that world.

TOMORROW
from the Musical Production ANNIE

Lyric by MARTIN CHARNIN
Music by CHARLES STROUSE

Moderately slow

The sun - 'll come out _____ to - mor - row,

bet your bot - tom dol - lar that to - mor - row _____ there'll be

sun! Jus' think - ing a - bout _____ to - mor - row

WHERE IS LOVE?
from the Columbia Pictures - Romulus Film OLIVER!

Words and Music by
LIONEL BART